The Order for the C

Holy Communi

also called

The Eucharist

and

The Lord's Supper

Church House Publishing

Order One

Published by   Church House Publishing
Church House
Great Smith Street
London SW1P 3NZ

Copyright ©   *The Archbishops' Council 2000*

First published 2000

0 7151 2023 9

All rights reserved. No part of this publication may be reproduced in any form or by any means, electronic or mechanical, including photocopying, recording, or any information storage and retrieval system, except as stated below, without written permission.

Texts for local use: the arrangements which apply to local editions of services cover reproduction on a non-commercial basis both for a single occasion and for repeated use. Details are available in the booklet *A Brief Guide to Liturgical Copyright* (see Copyright Information in *Common Worship: Services and Prayers for the Church of England* for further information).

Printed and bound by ArklePrint Ltd, Northampton
on 80 gsm Dutchman Ivory

Typeset in 9 on 12 point Gill Sans
by John Morgan and Shirley Thompson / Omnific
Designed by Derek Birdsall RDI

The material in this booklet is extracted from *Common Worship: Services and Prayers for the Church of England*. It comprises:

¶   the Order for the Celebration of Holy Communion: Order One;
¶   extracts from Supplementary Texts to Holy Communion;
¶   the Apostles' Creed;
¶   A Form of Preparation;
¶   Notes to Holy Communion Order One.

For other material, page references to *Common Worship: Services and Prayers for the Church of England* are supplied.

Pagination   This booklet has two sets of page numbers. The outer numbers are the booklet's own page numbers, while the inner numbers near the centre of most pages refer to the equivalent pages in *Common Worship: Services and Prayers for the Church of England*.

Contents

General Notes   iv

Order One

Structure   vi

1   **Order One**
Eucharistic Prayers   18
    Prayer A   18
    Prayer B   22
    Prayer C   25
    Prayer D   28
    Prayer E   30
    Prayer F   32
    Prayer G   35
    Prayer H   38

40   **Supplementary Texts**
Penitential Material   40
The Apostles' Creed   44
Prayers at the Preparation of the Table   45
Prayers after Communion   46

47   **A Form of Preparation**

52   **Notes**

57   **Authorization**

58   **Acknowledgements**

¶ General Notes

¶ Preparation

Careful devotional preparation before the service is recommended for every communicant. A Form of Preparation for public or private use is provided (page 47).

¶ Ministries

Holy Communion is celebrated by the whole people of God gathered for worship. The ministry of the members of the congregation is expressed through their active participation together in the words and actions of the service, but also by some of them reading the Scripture passages, leading the prayers of intercession, and, if authorized, assisting with the distribution of communion.

In some traditions the ministry of the deacon at Holy Communion has included some of the following elements: the bringing in of the Book of the Gospels, the invitation to confession, the reading of the Gospel, the preaching of the sermon when licensed to do so, a part in the prayers of intercession, the preparation of the table and the gifts, a part in the distribution, the ablutions and the dismissal.

The deacon's liturgical ministry provides an appropriate model for the ministry of an assisting priest, a Reader, or another episcopally authorized minister in a leadership ministry that complements that of the president.

The unity of the liturgy is served by the ministry of the president, who in presiding over the whole service holds word and sacrament together and draws the congregation into a worshipping community.

The president at Holy Communion (who, in accordance with the provisions of Canon B 12 'Of the Ministry of the Holy Communion', must have been episcopally ordained priest) expresses this ministry by saying the opening Greeting, the Absolution, the Collect, the Peace and the Blessing. The president must say the Eucharistic Prayer, break the consecrated bread and receive the sacrament on every occasion. When appropriate, the president may, after greeting the people, delegate the leadership of all or parts of the Gathering and the Liturgy of the Word to a deacon, Reader or other authorized lay person.

In the absence of a priest for the first part of the service, a deacon, Reader or other authorized lay person may lead the entire Gathering and Liturgy of the Word.

When the bishop is present, he normally presides over the whole service.

As provided in Canon B 18 the sermon shall be preached by a duly authorized minister, deaconess, Reader or lay worker or, at the invitation of the minister having the cure of souls and with the permission of the bishop, another person.

¶   **Communicant members of other Churches**

Baptized persons who are communicant members of other Churches which subscribe to the doctrine of the Holy Trinity and are in good standing in their own Church shall be admitted to Communion in accordance with Canon B 15A.

In preparing for the service, the president and other ministers should refer to the General Rules and the full range of Supplementary Texts and Seasonal Provisions to the Order for the Celebration of Holy Communion in Common Worship: Services and Prayers for the Church of England (pages 525 and 268–329) and the President's edition of Common Worship (pages 495–608).

For further Notes, see pages 52–56.

Order One

The people and the priest

¶ greet each other in the Lord's name

¶ confess their sins and are assured of God's forgiveness

¶ keep silence and pray a Collect

¶ proclaim and respond to the word of God

¶ pray for the Church and the world

¶ exchange the Peace

¶ prepare the table

¶ pray the Eucharistic Prayer

¶ break the bread

¶ receive communion

¶ depart with God's blessing

For Notes, see pages iv–v and 52–56.

Order One

¶ *The Gathering*

At the entry of the ministers a hymn may be sung.

The president may say

In the name of the Father,
and of the Son,
and of the Holy Spirit.

All   **Amen.**

The Greeting

The president greets the people

The Lord be with you

All   **and also with you.**

(or)

Grace, mercy and peace
from God our Father
and the Lord Jesus Christ
be with you

All   **and also with you.**

From Easter Day to Pentecost this acclamation follows

Alleluia. Christ is risen.

All   **He is risen indeed. Alleluia.**

Words of welcome or introduction may be said.

Prayer of Preparation

This prayer may be said

All **Almighty God,**
to whom all hearts are open,
all desires known,
and from whom no secrets are hidden:
cleanse the thoughts of our hearts
by the inspiration of your Holy Spirit,
that we may perfectly love you,
and worthily magnify your holy name;
through Christ our Lord.
Amen.

Prayers of Penitence

The Commandments, the Comfortable Words, the Beatitudes
(pages 40–43 and 48–50) or the following Summary of the Law
may be used

Our Lord Jesus Christ said:
The first commandment is this:
'Hear, O Israel, the Lord our God is the only Lord.
You shall love the Lord your God with all your heart,
with all your soul, with all your mind,
and with all your strength.'

The second is this: 'Love your neighbour as yourself.'
There is no other commandment greater than these.
On these two commandments hang all the law and the prophets.

All **Amen. Lord, have mercy.**

A minister uses a seasonal invitation to confession or these or other
suitable words

God so loved the world
that he gave his only Son Jesus Christ
to save us from our sins,
to be our advocate in heaven,
and to bring us to eternal life.

Let us confess our sins in penitence and faith,
firmly resolved to keep God's commandments
and to live in love and peace with all.

All **Almighty God, our heavenly Father,**
we have sinned against you
and against our neighbour
in thought and word and deed,
through negligence, through weakness,
through our own deliberate fault.
We are truly sorry
and repent of all our sins.
For the sake of your Son Jesus Christ,
who died for us,
forgive us all that is past
and grant that we may serve you in newness of life
to the glory of your name.
Amen.

(or)

All **Most merciful God,**
Father of our Lord Jesus Christ,
we confess that we have sinned
in thought, word and deed.
We have not loved you with our whole heart.
We have not loved our neighbours as ourselves.
In your mercy
forgive what we have been,
help us to amend what we are,
and direct what we shall be;
that we may do justly,
love mercy,
and walk humbly with you, our God.
Amen.

Or, with suitable penitential sentences, the Kyrie eleison may be used

Lord, have mercy.

All **Lord, have mercy.**

Christ, have mercy.

All **Christ, have mercy.**

Lord, have mercy.

All **Lord, have mercy.**

If another confession has already been used, the Kyrie eleison may be used without interpolation here or after the absolution.

The president says

Almighty God,
who forgives all who truly repent,
have mercy upon *you*,
pardon and deliver *you* from all *your* sins,
confirm and strengthen *you* in all goodness,
and keep *you* in life eternal;
through Jesus Christ our Lord.

All **Amen.**

Gloria in Excelsis

The Gloria in excelsis may be used

All   **Glory to God in the highest,**
and peace to his people on earth.

Lord God, heavenly King,
almighty God and Father,
we worship you, we give you thanks,
we praise you for your glory.

Lord Jesus Christ, only Son of the Father,
Lord God, Lamb of God,
you take away the sin of the world:
have mercy on us;
you are seated at the right hand of the Father:
receive our prayer.

For you alone are the Holy One,
you alone are the Lord,
you alone are the Most High, Jesus Christ,
with the Holy Spirit,
in the glory of God the Father.
Amen.

The Collect

The president introduces a period of silent prayer with the words
'Let us pray' or a more specific bidding.

The Collect is said, and all respond

All   **Amen.**

Readings

Either one or two readings from Scripture precede the Gospel reading.

At the end of each the reader may say

This is the word of the Lord.

All   **Thanks be to God.**

The psalm or canticle follows the first reading; other hymns and songs may be used between the readings.

Gospel Reading

An acclamation may herald the Gospel reading.

When the Gospel is announced the reader says

Hear the Gospel of our Lord Jesus Christ according to *N.*

All   **Glory to you, O Lord.**

At the end

This is the Gospel of the Lord.

All   **Praise to you, O Christ.**

Sermon

The Creed

On Sundays and Principal Holy Days an authorized translation of
the Nicene Creed is used, or on occasion the Apostles' Creed (page 44)
or an authorized Affirmation of Faith may be used (see pages 138–148
in Common Worship: Services and Prayers for the Church of England).

All   **We believe in one God,**
the Father, the Almighty,
maker of heaven and earth,
of all that is,
seen and unseen.

We believe in one Lord, Jesus Christ,
the only Son of God,
eternally begotten of the Father,
God from God, Light from Light,
true God from true God,
begotten, not made,
of one Being with the Father;
through him all things were made.
For us and for our salvation he came down from heaven,
was incarnate from the Holy Spirit and the Virgin Mary
and was made man.
For our sake he was crucified under Pontius Pilate;
he suffered death and was buried.
On the third day he rose again
in accordance with the Scriptures;
he ascended into heaven
and is seated at the right hand of the Father.
He will come again in glory to judge the living and the dead,
and his kingdom will have no end.

We believe in the Holy Spirit,
the Lord, the giver of life,
who proceeds from the Father and the Son,
who with the Father and the Son is worshipped and glorified,
who has spoken through the prophets.
We believe in one holy catholic and apostolic Church.
We acknowledge one baptism for the forgiveness of sins.
We look for the resurrection of the dead,
and the life of the world to come.
Amen.

Prayers of Intercession

One of the forms on pages 281–289 in Common Worship: Services and Prayers for the Church of England *or other suitable words may be used.*

The prayers usually include these concerns and may follow this sequence:

¶ *The Church of Christ*

¶ *Creation, human society, the Sovereign and those in authority*

¶ *The local community*

¶ *Those who suffer*

¶ *The communion of saints*

These responses may be used

Lord, in your mercy
All **hear our prayer.**

(or)

Lord, hear us.
All **Lord, graciously hear us.**

And at the end

Merciful Father,
All **accept these prayers
for the sake of your Son,
our Saviour Jesus Christ.
Amen.**

¶ *The Liturgy of the Sacrament*

The Peace

The president may introduce the Peace with a suitable sentence, and then says

The peace of the Lord be always with you

All **and also with you.**

These words may be added
Let us offer one another a sign of peace.

All may exchange a sign of peace.

Preparation of the Table
Taking of the Bread and Wine

A hymn may be sung.

The gifts of the people may be gathered and presented.

The table is prepared and bread and wine are placed upon it.

One or more of the prayers at the preparation of the table may be said.

The president takes the bread and wine.

The Eucharistic Prayer

An authorized Eucharistic Prayer is used (pages 18–39).

The president says

The Lord be with you   *(or)*   The Lord is here.

All   **and also with you.**   **His Spirit is with us.**

Lift up your hearts.

All   **We lift them to the Lord.**

Let us give thanks to the Lord our God.

All   **It is right to give thanks and praise.**

The president praises God for his mighty acts and all respond

All   **Holy, holy, holy Lord,**
       God of power and might,
       heaven and earth are full of your glory.
       Hosanna in the highest.
       [Blessed is he who comes in the name of the Lord.
       Hosanna in the highest.]

The president recalls the Last Supper,
and one of these four acclamations may be used

[Great is the mystery of faith:]   [Praise to you, Lord Jesus:]

All   **Christ has died:**   **Dying you destroyed**
       Christ is risen: **our death,**
       Christ will come again.   **rising you restored our life:**
                                     Lord Jesus, come in glory.

[Christ is the bread of life:]   [Jesus Christ is Lord:]

All   **When we eat this bread**   **Lord, by your cross and**
       and drink this cup,   **resurrection**
       we proclaim your death,   **you have set us free.**
         Lord Jesus,   **You are the Saviour of the**
       until you come in glory.   **world.**

The Prayer continues and leads into the doxology,
to which all respond boldly

All   **Amen.**

Prayer A

page 18

This response may be used

All **To you be glory and praise for ever.**

and the Prayer ends

All **Blessing and honour and glory and power
be yours for ever and ever.
Amen.**

Prayer D

page 28

These words are used

This is his/our story.
All **This is our song:
Hosanna in the highest.**

and the Prayer ends

All **Blessing and honour and glory and power
be yours for ever and ever.
Amen.**

Prayer F

page 32

These responses may be used

All **Amen. Lord, we believe.**

All **Amen. Come, Lord Jesus.**

All **Amen. Come, Holy Spirit.**

Prayer G

page 35

Prayer G ends

All **Blessing and honour and glory and power
be yours for ever and ever.
Amen.**

Prayer H

page 38

For Prayer H, see page 38.

The Lord's Prayer

As our Saviour taught us, so we pray

All   **Our Father in heaven,**
hallowed be your name,
your kingdom come,
your will be done,
on earth as in heaven.
Give us today our daily bread.
Forgive us our sins
as we forgive those who sin against us.
Lead us not into temptation
but deliver us from evil.
For the kingdom, the power,
and the glory are yours
now and for ever.
Amen.

(or)

Let us pray with confidence as our Saviour has taught us

All   **Our Father, who art in heaven,**
hallowed be thy name;
thy kingdom come;
thy will be done;
on earth as it is in heaven.
Give us this day our daily bread.
And forgive us our trespasses,
as we forgive those who trespass against us.
And lead us not into temptation;
but deliver us from evil.
For thine is the kingdom,
the power and the glory,
for ever and ever.
Amen.

Breaking of the Bread

The president breaks the consecrated bread.

We break this bread
to share in the body of Christ.

All **Though we are many, we are one body,
because we all share in one bread.**

(or)

Every time we eat this bread
and drink this cup,

All **we proclaim the Lord's death
until he comes.**

The Agnus Dei may be used as the bread is broken

All **Lamb of God,
you take away the sin of the world,
have mercy on us.**

**Lamb of God,
you take away the sin of the world,
have mercy on us.**

**Lamb of God,
you take away the sin of the world,
grant us peace.**

(or)

All **Jesus, Lamb of God,
have mercy on us.**

**Jesus, bearer of our sins,
have mercy on us.**

**Jesus, redeemer of the world,
grant us peace.**

Giving of Communion

Draw near with faith.
Receive the body of our Lord Jesus Christ
which he gave for you,
and his blood which he shed for you.
Eat and drink
in remembrance that he died for you,
and feed on him in your hearts
by faith with thanksgiving.

(or)

Jesus is the Lamb of God
who takes away the sin of the world.
Blessed are those who are called to his supper.

All **Lord, I am not worthy to receive you,**
but only say the word, and I shall be healed.

(or)

God's holy gifts
for God's holy people.

All **Jesus Christ is holy,**
Jesus Christ is Lord,
to the glory of God the Father.

or, from Easter Day to Pentecost

Alleluia. Christ our passover is sacrificed for us.

All **Therefore let us keep the feast. Alleluia.**

All **We do not presume**
to come to this your table, merciful Lord,
trusting in our own righteousness,
but in your manifold and great mercies.
We are not worthy
so much as to gather up the crumbs under your table.
But you are the same Lord
whose nature is always to have mercy.
Grant us therefore, gracious Lord,
so to eat the flesh of your dear Son Jesus Christ
and to drink his blood,
that our sinful bodies may be made clean by his body
and our souls washed through his most precious blood,
and that we may evermore dwell in him, and he in us.
Amen.

(or)

All **Most merciful Lord,**
your love compels us to come in.
Our hands were unclean,
our hearts were unprepared;
we were not fit
even to eat the crumbs from under your table.
But you, Lord, are the God of our salvation,
and share your bread with sinners.
So cleanse and feed us
with the precious body and blood of your Son,
that he may live in us and we in him;
and that we, with the whole company of Christ,
may sit and eat in your kingdom.
Amen.

The president and people receive communion.

Authorized words of distribution are used and the communicant replies

Amen.

During the distribution hymns and anthems may be sung.

If either or both of the consecrated elements are likely to prove insufficient, the president returns to the holy table and adds more, saying the words on page 296 in Common Worship: Services and Prayers for the Church of England.

Any consecrated bread and wine which is not required for purposes of communion is consumed at the end of the distribution or after the service.

Prayer after Communion

Silence is kept.

The Post Communion or another suitable prayer is said.

All may say one of these prayers

All **Almighty God,**
we thank you for feeding us
with the body and blood of your Son Jesus Christ.
Through him we offer you our souls and bodies
to be a living sacrifice.
Send us out
in the power of your Spirit
to live and work
to your praise and glory.
Amen.

(or)

All **Father of all,**
we give you thanks and praise,
that when we were still far off
you met us in your Son and brought us home.
Dying and living, he declared your love,
gave us grace, and opened the gate of glory.
May we who share Christ's body live his risen life;
we who drink his cup bring life to others;
we whom the Spirit lights give light to the world.
Keep us firm in the hope you have set before us,
so we and all your children shall be free,
and the whole earth live to praise your name;
through Christ our Lord.
Amen.

¶ *The Dismissal*

A hymn may be sung.

The president may use the seasonal blessing, or another suitable blessing

(or)

The peace of God,
which passes all understanding,
keep your hearts and minds
in the knowledge and love of God,
and of his Son Jesus Christ our Lord;
and the blessing of God almighty,
the Father, the Son, and the Holy Spirit,
be among you and remain with you always.

All **Amen.**

A minister says

Go in peace to love and serve the Lord.

All **In the name of Christ. Amen.**

(or)

Go in the peace of Christ.

All **Thanks be to God.**

or, from Easter Day to Pentecost

Go in the peace of Christ. Alleluia, alleluia.

All **Thanks be to God. Alleluia, alleluia.**

The ministers and people depart.

¶ *Eucharistic Prayers for use in Order One*

Proper Prefaces are to be found on pages 294 and 300–329 in Common Worship: Services and Prayers for the Church of England.

Prayer A

If an extended Preface is used, it replaces all words between the opening dialogue and the Sanctus.

The Lord be with you   *(or)*   The Lord is here.

All **and also with you.**   **His Spirit is with us.**

Lift up your hearts.

All **We lift them to the Lord.**

Let us give thanks to the Lord our God.

All **It is right to give thanks and praise.**

It is indeed right,
it is our duty and our joy,
at all times and in all places
to give you thanks and praise,
holy Father, heavenly King,
almighty and eternal God,
through Jesus Christ your Son our Lord.

The following may be omitted if a short Proper Preface is used

For he is your living Word;
through him you have created all things from the beginning,
and formed us in your own image.

[*All* **To you be glory and praise for ever.**]

Through him you have freed us from the slavery of sin,
giving him to be born of a woman and to die upon the cross;
you raised him from the dead
and exalted him to your right hand on high.

[*All* **To you be glory and praise for ever.**]

Through him you have sent upon us
your holy and life-giving Spirit,
and made us a people for your own possession.

[*All* **To you be glory and praise for ever.**]

Therefore with angels and archangels,
and with all the company of heaven,
we proclaim your great and glorious name,
for ever praising you and *saying:*

All **Holy, holy, holy Lord,**
God of power and might,
heaven and earth are full of your glory.
Hosanna in the highest.
[Blessed is he who comes in the name of the Lord.
Hosanna in the highest.]

Accept our praises, heavenly Father,
through your Son our Saviour Jesus Christ,
and as we follow his example and obey his command,
grant that by the power of your Holy Spirit
these gifts of bread and wine
may be to us his body and his blood;

who, in the same night that he was betrayed,
took bread and gave you thanks;
he broke it and gave it to his disciples, saying:
Take, eat; this is my body which is given for you;
do this in remembrance of me.

[*All* **To you be glory and praise for ever.**]

In the same way, after supper
he took the cup and gave you thanks;
he gave it to them, saying:
Drink this, all of you;
this is my blood of the new covenant,
which is shed for you and for many for the forgiveness of sins.
Do this, as often as you drink it,
in remembrance of me.

[*All* **To you be glory and praise for ever.**]

Therefore, heavenly Father,
we remember his offering of himself
made once for all upon the cross;
we proclaim his mighty resurrection and glorious ascension;
we look for the coming of your kingdom,
and with this bread and this cup
we make the memorial of Christ your Son our Lord.

One of these four acclamations is used

[Great is the mystery of faith:]
All **Christ has died:**
Christ is risen:
Christ will come again.

(or)

[Praise to you, Lord Jesus:]
All **Dying you destroyed our death,**
rising you restored our life:
Lord Jesus, come in glory.

(or)

[Christ is the bread of life:]
All **When we eat this bread and drink this cup,**
we proclaim your death, Lord Jesus,
until you come in glory.

(or)

[Jesus Christ is Lord:]
All **Lord, by your cross and resurrection**
you have set us free.
You are the Saviour of the world.

Accept through him, our great high priest,
this our sacrifice of thanks and praise,
and as we eat and drink these holy gifts
in the presence of your divine majesty,
renew us by your Spirit,
inspire us with your love
and unite us in the body of your Son,
Jesus Christ our Lord.

[*All*] **To you be glory and praise for ever.]**

Through him, and with him, and in him,
in the unity of the Holy Spirit,
with all who stand before you in earth and heaven,
we worship you, Father almighty,
in songs of everlasting praise:

All **Blessing and honour and glory and power
be yours for ever and ever.
Amen.**

The service continues with the Lord's Prayer on page 12.

Prayer B

If an extended Preface is used, it replaces all words between the opening dialogue and the Sanctus.

The Lord be with you   *(or)*   The Lord is here.
All **and also with you.**   **His Spirit is with us.**

Lift up your hearts.
All **We lift them to the Lord.**

Let us give thanks to the Lord our God.
All **It is right to give thanks and praise.**

Father, we give you thanks and praise
through your beloved Son Jesus Christ, your living Word,
through whom you have created all things;
who was sent by you in your great goodness to be our Saviour.

By the power of the Holy Spirit he took flesh;
as your Son, born of the blessed Virgin,
he lived on earth and went about among us;
he opened wide his arms for us on the cross;
he put an end to death by dying for us;
and revealed the resurrection by rising to new life;
so he fulfilled your will and won for you a holy people.

Short Proper Preface, when appropriate

Therefore with angels and archangels,
and with all the company of heaven,
we proclaim your great and glorious name,
for ever praising you and *saying*:

All **Holy, holy, holy Lord,**
God of power and might,
heaven and earth are full of your glory.
Hosanna in the highest.
[Blessed is he who comes in the name of the Lord.
Hosanna in the highest.]

Lord, you are holy indeed, the source of all holiness;
grant that by the power of your Holy Spirit,
and according to your holy will,
these gifts of bread and wine
may be to us the body and blood of our Lord Jesus Christ;

who, in the same night that he was betrayed,
took bread and gave you thanks;
he broke it and gave it to his disciples, saying:
Take, eat; this is my body which is given for you;
do this in remembrance of me.

In the same way, after supper
he took the cup and gave you thanks;
he gave it to them, saying:
Drink this, all of you;
this is my blood of the new covenant,
which is shed for you and for many for the forgiveness of sins.
Do this, as often as you drink it,
in remembrance of me.

One of these four acclamations is used

[Great is the mystery of faith:]

All **Christ has died:**
Christ is risen:
Christ will come again.

(or)

[Praise to you, Lord Jesus:]

All **Dying you destroyed our death,**
rising you restored our life:
Lord Jesus, come in glory.

(or)

[Christ is the bread of life:]

All **When we eat this bread and drink this cup,**
we proclaim your death, Lord Jesus,
until you come in glory.

(or)

[Jesus Christ is Lord:]

All **Lord, by your cross and resurrection**
you have set us free.
You are the Saviour of the world.

And so, Father, calling to mind his death on the cross,
his perfect sacrifice made once for the sins of the whole world;
rejoicing in his mighty resurrection and glorious ascension,
and looking for his coming in glory,
we celebrate this memorial of our redemption.
As we offer you this our sacrifice of praise and thanksgiving,
we bring before you this bread and this cup
and we thank you for counting us worthy
to stand in your presence and serve you.

Send the Holy Spirit on your people
and gather into one in your kingdom
all who share this one bread and one cup,
so that we, in the company of [*N and*] all the saints,
may praise and glorify you for ever,
through Jesus Christ our Lord;

by whom, and with whom, and in whom,
in the unity of the Holy Spirit,
all honour and glory be yours, almighty Father,
for ever and ever.

All **Amen.**

The service continues with the Lord's Prayer on page 12.

Prayer C

The Lord be with you *(or)*   The Lord is here.
All and also with you.   **His Spirit is with us.**

Lift up your hearts.
All We lift them to the Lord.

Let us give thanks to the Lord our God.
All It is right to give thanks and praise.

It is indeed right,
it is our duty and our joy,
at all times and in all places
to give you thanks and praise,
holy Father, heavenly King,
almighty and eternal God,
through Jesus Christ our Lord.

Short Proper Preface, when appropriate

[or, when there is no Proper Preface

For he is our great high priest,
who has loosed us from our sins
and has made us to be a royal priesthood to you,
our God and Father.]

Therefore with angels and archangels,
and with all the company of heaven,
we proclaim your great and glorious name,
for ever praising you and *saying*:

All Holy, holy, holy Lord,
God of power and might,
heaven and earth are full of your glory.
Hosanna in the highest.
[Blessed is he who comes in the name of the Lord.
Hosanna in the highest.]

All glory be to you, our heavenly Father,
who, in your tender mercy,
gave your only Son our Saviour Jesus Christ
to suffer death upon the cross for our redemption;
who made there by his one oblation of himself once offered
a full, perfect and sufficient sacrifice, oblation and satisfaction
for the sins of the whole world;
he instituted, and in his holy gospel commanded us to continue,
a perpetual memory of his precious death until he comes again.

Hear us, merciful Father, we humbly pray,
and grant that, by the power of your Holy Spirit,
we receiving these gifts of your creation, this bread and this wine,
according to your Son our Saviour Jesus Christ's holy institution,
in remembrance of his death and passion,
may be partakers of his most blessed body and blood;

who, in the same night that he was betrayed,
took bread and gave you thanks;
he broke it and gave it to his disciples, saying:
Take, eat; this is my body which is given for you;
do this in remembrance of me.

In the same way, after supper
he took the cup and gave you thanks;
he gave it to them, saying:
Drink this, all of you;
this is my blood of the new covenant,
which is shed for you and for many for the forgiveness of sins.
Do this, as often as you drink it,
in remembrance of me.

One of these four acclamations is used

[Great is the mystery of faith:]

All **Christ has died:**
Christ is risen:
Christ will come again.

[Praise to you, Lord Jesus:]

Dying you destroyed
our death,
rising you restored our life:
Lord Jesus, come in glory.

[Christ is the bread of life:]

All **When we eat this bread**
and drink this cup,
we proclaim your death,
Lord Jesus,
until you come in glory.

[Jesus Christ is Lord:]

Lord, by your cross and
resurrection
you have set us free.
You are the Saviour of the
world.

Therefore, Lord and heavenly Father,
in remembrance of the precious death and passion,
the mighty resurrection and glorious ascension
of your dear Son Jesus Christ,
we offer you through him this our sacrifice of praise
    and thanksgiving.

Grant that by his merits and death,
and through faith in his blood,
we and all your Church may receive forgiveness of our sins
and all other benefits of his passion.
Although we are unworthy, through our manifold sins,
to offer you any sacrifice,
yet we pray that you will accept this
the duty and service that we owe.
Do not weigh our merits, but pardon our offences,
and fill us all who share in this holy communion
with your grace and heavenly blessing;

through Jesus Christ our Lord,
by whom, and with whom, and in whom,
in the unity of the Holy Spirit,
all honour and glory be yours, almighty Father,
for ever and ever.

All **Amen.**

The service continues with the Lord's Prayer on page 12.

Prayer D

The Lord be with you   *(or)*   The Lord is here.
All **and also with you.**   **His Spirit is with us.**

Lift up your hearts.
All **We lift them to the Lord.**

Let us give thanks to the Lord our God.
All **It is right to give thanks and praise.**

Almighty God, good Father to us all,
your face is turned towards your world.
In love you gave us Jesus your Son
to rescue us from sin and death.
Your Word goes out to call us home
     to the city where angels sing your praise.
We join with them in heaven's song:

All **Holy, holy, holy Lord,**
God of power and might,
heaven and earth are full of your glory.
Hosanna in the highest.
[Blessed is he who comes in the name of the Lord.
Hosanna in the highest.]

Father of all, we give you thanks
     for every gift that comes from heaven.

To the darkness Jesus came as your light.
With signs of faith and words of hope
he touched untouchables with love and washed the guilty clean.

This is his story.
All **This is our song:**
Hosanna in the highest.

The crowds came out to see your Son,
     yet at the end they turned on him.
On the night he was betrayed
he came to table with his friends
     to celebrate the freedom of your people.

This is his story.
All **This is our song:**
Hosanna in the highest.

Jesus blessed you, Father, for the food;
he took bread, gave thanks, broke it and said:
This is my body, given for you all.
Jesus then gave thanks for the wine;
he took the cup, gave it and said:
This is my blood, shed for you all
    for the forgiveness of sins.
Do this in remembrance of me.

This is our story.

All **This is our song:
Hosanna in the highest.**

Therefore, Father, with this bread and this cup
we celebrate the cross
on which he died to set us free.
Defying death he rose again
and is alive with you to plead for us and all the world.

This is our story.

All **This is our song:
Hosanna in the highest.**

Send your Spirit on us now
that by these gifts we may feed on Christ
    with opened eyes and hearts on fire.

May we and all who share this food
offer ourselves to live for you
and be welcomed at your feast in heaven
    where all creation worships you,
Father, Son and Holy Spirit:

All **Blessing and honour and glory and power
be yours for ever and ever.
Amen.**

The service continues with the Lord's Prayer on page 12.

The Lord be with you   *(or)*   The Lord is here.

All **and also with you.**   **His Spirit is with us.**

Lift up your hearts.

All **We lift them to the Lord.**

Let us give thanks to the Lord our God.

All **It is right to give thanks and praise.**

Here follows an extended Preface or the following

Father, you made the world and love your creation.
You gave your Son Jesus Christ to be our Saviour.
His dying and rising have set us free from sin and death.
And so we gladly thank you,
with saints and angels praising you, and *saying*:

All **Holy, holy, holy Lord,**
God of power and might,
heaven and earth are full of your glory.
Hosanna in the highest.
[Blessed is he who comes in the name of the Lord.
Hosanna in the highest.]

We praise and bless you, loving Father,
through Jesus Christ, our Lord;
and as we obey his command,
send your Holy Spirit,
that broken bread and wine outpoured
may be for us the body and blood of your dear Son.

On the night before he died he had supper with his friends
and, taking bread, he praised you.
He broke the bread, gave it to them and said:
Take, eat; this is my body which is given for you;
do this in remembrance of me.

When supper was ended he took the cup of wine.
Again he praised you, gave it to them and said:
Drink this, all of you;
this is my blood of the new covenant,
which is shed for you and for many for the forgiveness of sins.
Do this, as often as you drink it, in remembrance of me.

So, Father, we remember all that Jesus did,
in him we plead with confidence his sacrifice
        made once for all upon the cross.

Bringing before you the bread of life and cup of salvation,
we proclaim his death and resurrection
until he comes in glory.

One of these four acclamations is used

[Great is the mystery of faith:]

All   **Christ has died:**
Christ is risen:
Christ will come again.

[Praise to you, Lord Jesus:]
Dying you destroyed
        our death,
rising you restored our life:
Lord Jesus, come in glory.

[Christ is the bread of life:]

All   **When we eat this bread**
        and drink this cup,
we proclaim your death,
        Lord Jesus,
until you come in glory.

[Jesus Christ is Lord:]
Lord, by your cross and
        resurrection
you have set us free.
You are the Saviour of the
        world.

Lord of all life,
help us to work together for that day
when your kingdom comes
and justice and mercy will be seen in all the earth.

Look with favour on your people,
gather us in your loving arms
and bring us with [N and] all the saints
to feast at your table in heaven.

Through Christ, and with Christ, and in Christ,
in the unity of the Holy Spirit,
all honour and glory are yours, O loving Father,
for ever and ever.

All   **Amen.**

The service continues with the Lord's Prayer on page 12.

Prayer F

The Lord be with you   *(or)*   The Lord is here.
All   **and also with you.**   **His Spirit is with us.**

Lift up your hearts.
All   **We lift them to the Lord.**

Let us give thanks to the Lord our God.
All   **It is right to give thanks and praise.**

You are worthy of our thanks and praise,
Lord God of truth,
for by the breath of your mouth
you have spoken your word,
and all things have come into being.

You fashioned us in your image
and placed us in the garden of your delight.
Though we chose the path of rebellion
you would not abandon your own.

Again and again you drew us into your covenant of grace.
You gave your people the law and taught us by your prophets
to look for your reign of justice, mercy and peace.

As we watch for the signs of your kingdom on earth,
we echo the song of the angels in heaven,
evermore praising you and *saying*:

All   **Holy, holy, holy Lord,**
God of power and might,
heaven and earth are full of your glory.
Hosanna in the highest.
[Blessed is he who comes in the name of the Lord.
Hosanna in the highest.]

Lord God, you are the most holy one,
enthroned in splendour and light,
yet in the coming of your Son Jesus Christ
you reveal the power of your love
made perfect in our human weakness.

[All   **Amen. Lord, we believe.**]

Embracing our humanity,
Jesus showed us the way of salvation;
loving us to the end,
he gave himself to death for us;
dying for his own,
he set us free from the bonds of sin,
that we might rise and reign with him in glory.

[*All*] **Amen. Lord, we believe.**]

On the night he gave up himself for us all
he took bread and gave you thanks;
he broke it and gave it to his disciples, saying:
Take, eat; this is my body which is given for you;
do this in remembrance of me.

[*All*] **Amen. Lord, we believe.**]

In the same way, after supper
he took the cup and gave you thanks;
he gave it to them, saying:
Drink this, all of you; this is my blood of the new covenant
which is shed for you and for many for the forgiveness of sins.
Do this, as often as you drink it, in remembrance of me.

[*All*] **Amen. Lord, we believe.**]

Therefore we proclaim the death that he suffered on the cross,
we celebrate his resurrection, his bursting from the tomb,
we rejoice that he reigns at your right hand on high
and we long for his coming in glory.

[*All*] **Amen. Come, Lord Jesus.**]

As we recall the one, perfect sacrifice of our redemption,
Father, by your Holy Spirit let these gifts of your creation
be to us the body and blood of our Lord Jesus Christ;
form us into the likeness of Christ
and make us a perfect offering in your sight.

[*All*] **Amen. Come, Holy Spirit.**]

Look with favour on your people
and in your mercy hear the cry of our hearts.
Bless the earth,
heal the sick,
let the oppressed go free
and fill your Church with power from on high.

[*All*   **Amen. Come, Holy Spirit.**]

Gather your people from the ends of the earth
to feast with [*N and*] all your saints
at the table in your kingdom,
where the new creation is brought to perfection
in Jesus Christ our Lord;

by whom, and with whom, and in whom,
in the unity of the Holy Spirit,
all honour and glory be yours, almighty Father,
for ever and ever.

All   **Amen.**

The service continues with the Lord's Prayer on page 12.

Prayer G

The Lord be with you   *(or)*   The Lord is here.
All **and also with you.**   **His Spirit is with us.**

Lift up your hearts.
All **We lift them to the Lord.**

Let us give thanks to the Lord our God.
All **It is right to give thanks and praise.**

Blessed are you, Lord God,
our light and our salvation;
to you be glory and praise for ever.

From the beginning you have created all things
and all your works echo the silent music of your praise.
In the fullness of time you made us in your image,
the crown of all creation.

You give us breath and speech, that with angels and archangels
and all the powers of heaven
we may find a voice to sing your praise:

All **Holy, holy, holy Lord,**
God of power and might,
heaven and earth are full of your glory.
Hosanna in the highest.
[Blessed is he who comes in the name of the Lord.
Hosanna in the highest.]

How wonderful the work of your hands, O Lord.
As a mother tenderly gathers her children,
you embraced a people as your own.
When they turned away and rebelled
your love remained steadfast.

From them you raised up Jesus our Saviour, born of Mary,
to be the living bread,
in whom all our hungers are satisfied.

He offered his life for sinners,
and with a love stronger than death
he opened wide his arms on the cross.

On the night before he died,
he came to supper with his friends
and, taking bread, he gave you thanks.
He broke it and gave it to them, saying:
Take, eat; this is my body which is given for you;
do this in remembrance of me.

At the end of supper, taking the cup of wine,
he gave you thanks, and said:
Drink this, all of you; this is my blood of the new covenant,
which is shed for you and for many for the forgiveness of sins.
Do this, as often as you drink it, in remembrance of me.

One of these four acclamations is used

[Great is the mystery of faith:]

All **Christ has died:**
Christ is risen:
Christ will come again.

(or)

[Praise to you, Lord Jesus:]

All **Dying you destroyed our death,**
rising you restored our life:
Lord Jesus, come in glory.

(or)

[Christ is the bread of life:]

All **When we eat this bread and drink this cup**
we proclaim your death, Lord Jesus,
until you come in glory.

(or)

[Jesus Christ is Lord:]

All **Lord, by your cross and resurrection**
you have set us free.
You are the Saviour of the world.

Father, we plead with confidence
his sacrifice made once for all upon the cross;
we remember his dying and rising in glory,
and we rejoice that he intercedes for us at your right hand.

Pour out your Holy Spirit as we bring before you
these gifts of your creation;
may they be for us the body and blood of your dear Son.

As we eat and drink these holy things in your presence,
form us in the likeness of Christ,
and build us into a living temple to your glory.

[Remember, Lord, your Church in every land.
Reveal her unity, guard her faith,
and preserve her in peace ...]

Bring us at the last with [N and] all the saints
to the vision of that eternal splendour
for which you have created us;
through Jesus Christ, our Lord,
by whom, with whom, and in whom,
with all who stand before you in earth and heaven,
we worship you, Father almighty, in songs of everlasting praise:

All **Blessing and honour and glory and power
be yours for ever and ever.
Amen.**

The service continues with the Lord's Prayer on page 12.

Prayer H

The Lord be with you   *(or)*   The Lord is here.

All   **and also with you.**   **His Spirit is with us.**

Lift up your hearts.

All   **We lift them to the Lord.**

Let us give thanks to the Lord our God.

All   **It is right to give thanks and praise.**

It is right to praise you, Father, Lord of all creation;
in your love you made us for yourself.

When we turned away
you did not reject us,
but came to meet us in your Son.

All   **You embraced us as your children**
and welcomed us to sit and eat with you.

In Christ you shared our life
that we might live in him and he in us.

All   **He opened his arms of love upon the cross**
and made for all the perfect sacrifice for sin.

On the night he was betrayed,
at supper with his friends
he took bread, and gave you thanks;
he broke it and gave it to them, saying:
Take, eat; this is my body which is given for you;
do this in remembrance of me.

All   **Father, we do this in remembrance of him:**
his body is the bread of life.

At the end of supper, taking the cup of wine,
he gave you thanks, and said:
Drink this, all of you; this is my blood of the new covenant,
which is shed for you for the forgiveness of sins;
do this in remembrance of me.

All   **Father, we do this in remembrance of him:**
his blood is shed for all.

As we proclaim his death and celebrate his rising in glory,
send your Holy Spirit that this bread and this wine
may be to us the body and blood of your dear Son.

All **As we eat and drink these holy gifts
make us one in Christ, our risen Lord.**

With your whole Church throughout the world
we offer you this sacrifice of praise
and lift our voice to join the eternal song of heaven:

All **Holy, holy, holy Lord,
God of power and might,
Heaven and earth are full of your glory.
Hosanna in the highest.**

The service continues with the Lord's Prayer on page 12.

Supplementary Texts

¶ *Penitential Material*

The Commandments

I

At the discretion of the minister, responses may be used only after the fourth and tenth Commandments, or only after the tenth Commandment.

God spoke these words and said: I am the Lord your God
[who brought you out of the land of Egypt, out of the house of slaver
you shall have no other gods but me.

All **Lord, have mercy upon us,**
and incline our hearts to keep this law.

You shall not make for yourself any idol,
whether in the form of anything that is in heaven above,
or that is on the earth beneath, or that is in the water under the ear
You shall not bow down to them or worship them.
[For I the Lord your God am a jealous God,
punishing children for the iniquity of parents
to the third and the fourth generation of those who reject me,
but showing steadfast love to a thousand generations of those
    who love me
and keep my commandments.]

All **Lord, have mercy upon us,**
and incline our hearts to keep this law.

You shall not take the name of the Lord your God in vain
[for the Lord will not hold him guiltless who takes his name in vain].

All **Lord, have mercy upon us,**
and incline our hearts to keep this law.

Remember the Sabbath day, and keep it holy.
For six days you shall labour and do all your work.
But the seventh day is a Sabbath to the Lord your God.
[You shall not do any work –
you, your son or your daughter,
your slaves, your livestock,
or the foreigner who lives among you.
For in six days the Lord made heaven and earth,
the sea, and all that is in them,
but rested the seventh day;
therefore the Lord blessed the seventh day and consecrated it.]

All **Lord, have mercy upon us,
and incline our hearts to keep this law.**

Honour your father and your mother
[so that your days may be long in the land
that the Lord your God is giving you].

All **Lord, have mercy upon us,
and incline our hearts to keep this law.**

You shall not murder.

All **Lord, have mercy upon us,
and incline our hearts to keep this law.**

You shall not commit adultery.

All **Lord, have mercy upon us,
and incline our hearts to keep this law.**

You shall not steal.

All **Lord, have mercy upon us,
and incline our hearts to keep this law.**

You shall not bear false witness [against your neighbour].

All **Lord, have mercy upon us,
and incline our hearts to keep this law.**

You shall not covet [your neighbour's house;
you shall not covet your neighbour's wife, or slaves, or ox, or donkey,
or anything that belongs to your neighbour].

All **Lord, have mercy upon us,
and write all these your laws in our hearts.**

2

Hear these commandments which God has given to his people,
and examine your hearts.

I am the Lord your God: you shall have no other gods but me.
You shall love the Lord your God with all your heart,
with all your soul, with all your mind, and with all your strength.

All **Amen. Lord, have mercy.**

You shall not make for yourself any idol.
God is spirit, and those who worship him must worship in spirit
        and in truth.

All **Amen. Lord, have mercy.**

You shall not dishonour the name of the Lord your God.
You shall worship him with awe and reverence.

All **Amen. Lord, have mercy.**

Remember the Sabbath and keep it holy.
Christ is risen from the dead: set your minds on things that are
above, not on things that are on the earth.

All **Amen. Lord, have mercy.**

Honour your father and mother.
Live as servants of God; let us work for the good of all,
especially members of the household of faith.

All **Amen. Lord, have mercy.**

You shall not commit murder.
Live peaceably with all; overcome evil with good.

All **Amen. Lord, have mercy.**

You shall not commit adultery.
Know that your body is a temple of the Holy Spirit.

All **Amen. Lord, have mercy.**

You shall not steal.
Be honest in all that you do, and care for those in need.

All **Amen. Lord, have mercy.**

You shall not be a false witness.
Let everyone speak the truth.

All **Amen. Lord, have mercy.**

You shall not covet anything which belongs to your neighbour.
Remember the words of the Lord Jesus:

'It is more blessed to give than to receive.'

Love your neighbour as yourself, for love is the fulfilling of the law.

All **Amen. Lord, have mercy.**

*For another form of the Commandments and forms of the
Comfortable Words and the Beatitudes, see pages 48–50.*

Confessions

*For other authorized confessions, see pages 123–134 and 277–278 in
Common Worship: Services and Prayers for the Church of England.*

1

All **Father eternal, giver of light and grace,**
we have sinned against you and against our neighbour,
in what we have thought,
in what we have said and done,
through ignorance, through weakness,
through our own deliberate fault.
We have wounded your love,
and marred your image in us.
We are sorry and ashamed,
and repent of all our sins.
For the sake of your Son Jesus Christ,
who died for us,
forgive us all that is past;
and lead us out from darkness
to walk as children of light.
Amen.

2

All **Almighty God, our heavenly Father,**
we have sinned against you,
through our own fault,
in thought, and word, and deed,
and in what we have left undone.
We are heartily sorry,
and repent of all our sins.
For your Son our Lord Jesus Christ's sake,
forgive us all that is past;
and grant that we may serve you in newness of life
to the glory of your name.
Amen.

¶ The Apostles' Creed

The origin of the Apostles' Creed is the profession of faith made at baptism. This association may have implications for the occasion when it is used at Holy Communion.

All **I believe in God, the Father almighty,
creator of heaven and earth.**

**I believe in Jesus Christ, his only Son, our Lord,
who was conceived by the Holy Spirit,
born of the Virgin Mary,
suffered under Pontius Pilate,
was crucified, died, and was buried;
he descended to the dead.
On the third day he rose again;
he ascended into heaven,
he is seated at the right hand of the Father,
and he will come to judge the living and the dead.**

**I believe in the Holy Spirit,
the holy catholic Church,
the communion of saints,
the forgiveness of sins,
the resurrection of the body,
and the life everlasting.
Amen.**

For other forms of the Creeds and authorized Affirmations of Faith, see pages 139–152 in Common Worship: Services and Prayers for the Church of England.

¶ *Prayers at the Preparation of the Table*

Yours, Lord, is the greatness, the power,
the glory, the splendour, and the majesty;
for everything in heaven and on earth is yours.

All **All things come from you,**
and of your own do we give you.

*In the following prayer, the texts for single voice need not be spoken
by the president. It will sometimes be appropriate to ask children
to speak them.*

With this bread that we bring

All **we shall remember Jesus.**

With this wine that we bring

All **we shall remember Jesus.**

Bread for his body,
wine for his blood,
gifts from God to his table we bring.

All **We shall remember Jesus.**

For further prayers, see pages 291–293 in Common Worship:
Services and Prayers for the Church of England.

The response to prayers which begin 'Blessed…' is
Blessed be God for ever.

¶ *Prayers after Communion*

1

All **We thank you, Lord,
that you have fed us in this sacrament,
united us with Christ,
and given us a foretaste of the heavenly banquet
prepared for all peoples.
Amen.**

2

All **Faithful God,
in baptism you have adopted us as your children,
made us members of the body of Christ
and chosen us as inheritors of your kingdom:
we thank you that in this Eucharist
you renew your promises within us,
empower us by your Spirit to witness and to serve,
and send us out as disciples of your Son,
Jesus Christ our Lord.
Amen.**

3

All **You have opened to us the Scriptures, O Christ,
and you have made yourself known
     in the breaking of the bread.
Abide with us, we pray,
that, blessed by your royal presence,
we may walk with you
all the days of our life,
and at its end behold you
in the glory of the eternal Trinity,
one God for ever and ever.
Amen.**

For Post Communions, see pages 298 and 375–447 in
Common Worship: Services and Prayers for the Church of England.

A Form of Preparation

This form may be used in any of three ways.

*It may be used by individuals as part of their preparation
for Holy Communion.*

*It may be used corporately on suitable occasions within Holy Communion
where it replaces the sections entitled 'Prayer of Preparation' and
'Prayers of Penitence'.*

*It may be used as a separate service of preparation. When used in this
way, there should be added at the beginning a greeting and at the end
the Peace and the Lord's Prayer. Hymns, psalms and other suitable
liturgical material may also be included.*

Come, Holy Ghost *(Veni creator Spiritus)*

All   **Come, Holy Ghost, our souls inspire,
And lighten with celestial fire;
Thou the anointing Spirit art,
Who dost thy sevenfold gifts impart.**

**Thy blessed unction from above
Is comfort, life and fire of love;
Enable with perpetual light
The dullness of our blinded sight.**

**Anoint and cheer our soiled face
With the abundance of thy grace;
Keep far our foes, give peace at home;
Where thou art guide no ill can come.**

**Teach us to know the Father, Son,
And thee, of Both, to be but One;
That through the ages all along
This may be our endless song:**

**Praise to thy eternal merit,
Father, Son and Holy Spirit.
Amen.**

Exhortation

As we gather at the Lord's table we must recall the promises and
warnings given to us in the Scriptures and so examine ourselves and
repent of our sins. We should give thanks to God for his redemption
of the world through his Son Jesus Christ and, as we remember
Christ's death for us and receive the pledge of his love, resolve
to serve him in holiness and righteousness all the days of our life.

The Commandments

Hear the commandments which God has given to his people,
and examine your hearts.

I am the Lord your God: you shall have no other gods but me.

All **Amen. Lord, have mercy.**

You shall not make for yourself any idol.

All **Amen. Lord, have mercy.**

You shall not dishonour the name of the Lord your God.

All **Amen. Lord, have mercy.**

Remember the Sabbath and keep it holy.

All **Amen. Lord, have mercy.**

Honour your father and your mother.

All **Amen. Lord, have mercy.**

You shall not commit murder.

All **Amen. Lord, have mercy.**

You shall not commit adultery.

All **Amen. Lord, have mercy.**

You shall not steal.

All **Amen. Lord, have mercy.**

You shall not bear false witness against your neighbour.

All **Amen. Lord, have mercy.**

You shall not covet anything which belongs to your neighbour.

All **Amen. Lord, have mercy upon us**
and write all these your laws in our hearts.

Or one of the forms of the Commandments in the Supplementary Texts
(pages 40–43) may be used.

Or, in place of the Commandments, one of these texts may be used.

Summary of the Law

Our Lord Jesus Christ said:
The first commandment is this:
'Hear, O Israel, the Lord our God is the only Lord.
You shall love the Lord your God with all your heart,
with all your soul, with all your mind,
and with all your strength.'

The second is this: 'Love your neighbour as yourself.'
There is no other commandment greater than these.
On these two commandments hang all the law and the prophets.

All **Amen. Lord, have mercy**.

(or)

The Comfortable Words

Hear the words of comfort our Saviour Christ says
to all who truly turn to him:

Come to me, all who labour and are heavy laden,
and I will give you rest. *Matthew 11.28*

God so loved the world that he gave his only-begotten Son,
that whoever believes in him should not perish
but have eternal life. *John 3.16*

Hear what Saint Paul says:
This saying is true, and worthy of full acceptance,
that Christ Jesus came into the world to save sinners. *1 Timothy 1.15*

Hear what Saint John says:
If anyone sins, we have an advocate with the Father,
Jesus Christ the righteous;
and he is the propitiation for our sins. *1 John 2.1, 2*

(or)

The Beatitudes

Let us hear our Lord's blessing on those who follow him.

Blessed are the poor in spirit,
for theirs is the kingdom of heaven.

Blessed are those who mourn,
for they shall be comforted.

Blessed are the meek,
for they shall inherit the earth.

Blessed are those who hunger and thirst after righteousness,
for they shall be satisfied.

Blessed are the merciful,
for they shall obtain mercy.

Blessed are the pure in heart,
for they shall see God.

Blessed are the peacemakers,
for they shall be called children of God.

Blessed are those who suffer persecution for righteousness' sake,
for theirs is the kingdom of heaven.

Silence for Reflection

Confession

All   **Father eternal, giver of light and grace,**
we have sinned against you and against our neighbour,
in what we have thought,
in what we have said and done,
through ignorance, through weakness,
through our own deliberate fault.
We have wounded your love
and marred your image in us.
We are sorry and ashamed
and repent of all our sins.
For the sake of your Son Jesus Christ,
who died for us,
forgive us all that is past
and lead us out from darkness
to walk as children of light.
Amen.

Or another authorized confession may be used.

Absolution

Almighty God, our heavenly Father,
who in his great mercy
has promised forgiveness of sins
to all those who with heartfelt repentance and true faith
    turn to him:
have mercy on *you*;
pardon and deliver *you* from all *your* sins;
confirm and strengthen *you* in all goodness;
and bring *you* to everlasting life;
through Jesus Christ our Lord.

All   **Amen.**

Notes

*The use of a lighter typeface for some texts reflects a decision of the
General Synod to give more weight to one choice within a range of option*

1   **Posture**
    Local custom may be followed and developed in relation to posture
    The people should stand for the reading of the Gospel, for the Cree
    for the Peace and for the Dismissal. Any changes in posture during
    the Eucharistic Prayer should not detract from the essential unity of
    that prayer. It is appropriate that, on occasions, the congregation
    should kneel for prayers of penitence.

2   **Traditional Texts**
    In addition to the places where they are printed in the service,
    traditional versions of texts may be used.

3   **Hymns, Psalms, Canticles, the Collection and Presentation
    of the Offerings of the People, and the Preparation of the Tab**
    Points are indicated for these, but they may occur elsewhere.

4   **Sentences**
    Sentences of Scripture appropriate to the season and the place
    in the service may be used as part of the president's greeting, in
    the Invitation to Confession, at the Peace, before the gifts of the
    people are collected and after the distribution of communion
    (from Easter Day to Pentecost 'Alleluia' is appropriately added
    to such sentences).

5   **Acclamations**
    Acclamations, which may include congregational response (such as
    'The Lord is here: his Spirit is with us' and 'Christ is risen: he is risen
    indeed') may be used at appropriate points in the service (with
    'Alleluia' except in Lent). Acclamations for use before the Gospel
    are provided on pages 280 and 300–329 in *Common Worship:
    Services and Prayers for the Church of England.*

6   **Entry**
    At the entry of the ministers, a Bible or Book of the Gospels may be
    carried into the assembly.

7   **Greetings**
In addition to the points where greetings are provided, at other
suitable points (e.g. before the Gospel and before the blessing or
dismissal), the greeting 'The Lord be with you' with its response
'and also with you' may be used.

8   **Silence**
Silence is particularly appropriate within the Prayers of Penitence
and of Intercession, before the Collect, in response to the reading of
the Scriptures, after the Eucharistic Prayer and after the distribution.

9   **Notices**
Banns of marriage and other notices may be published before the
Gathering (if possible by a minister other than the president), before
the Prayers of Intercession or before the Dismissal.

10   **The Prayers of Penitence**
This section may be transposed to a later point in the service as a
response to the Liturgy of the Word. In the special seasonal rites for
certain days it is particularly appropriate at the later point.

On certain occasions, for a special service, this section may
precede the opening hymn and greeting. A Form of Preparation is
provided on page 47.

The Invitation to Confession may take the form of the Summary
of the Law, the Commandments, the Beatitudes, the Comfortable
Words or the Exhortation.

When the Kyrie eleison is used as a confession, short penitential
sentences are inserted between the petitions, suitable for seasons
or themes. This form of confession should not be the norm on
Sundays.

Authorized alternative forms of confession and absolution may
be used in place of those in the main text (see pages 276–279 and
123–137 in *Common Worship: Services and Prayers for the Church of
England*).

11   **The Gloria in Excelsis**
This canticle may be omitted during Advent and Lent, and on
weekdays which are not Principal Holy Days or Festivals.
See also Note 3.

12 The Readings

The readings at Holy Communion are governed by authorized lectionary provision and are not a matter for local decision except where that provision permits.

Whenever possible, all three readings are used at Holy Communion on Sundays. When only two are read, the minister should ensure that, in any year, a balance is maintained between readings from the Old and New Testaments in the choice of the first reading. The psalm provided relates to the first reading in the lectionary. Where possible it should be used after that reading.

When announcing the Gospel, if it is desired to give book, chapter and verse or page number, the reader may do this informally before saying 'Hear the Gospel of our Lord Jesus Christ according to *N*.'

13 The Sermon

The sermon is an integral part of the Liturgy of the Word. A sermon should normally be preached at all celebrations on Sundays and Principal Holy Days.

The sermon may on occasion include less formal exposition of Scripture, the use of drama, interviews, discussion and audio-visual aids.

14 The Creed

The Creed may be preceded by the president saying 'Let us declare our faith in God, Father, Son and Holy Spirit'.

15 The Prayers of Intercession

Intercession frequently arises out of thanksgiving; nevertheless these prayers are primarily prayers of intercession. They are normally broadly based, expressing a concern for the whole of God's world and the ministry of the whole Church.

Several forms of intercession are provided (see pages 281–287 in *Common Worship: Services and Prayers for the Church of England*); other suitable forms may be used. They need not always conform to the sequence indicated.

Prayer for the nation is properly focused in prayer for the sovereign by name, and prayer for the Church in prayer for the bishop of the diocese by name.

The Supplementary Texts provide a number of Collects and other endings to conclude intercession (see pages 288–289 in *Common Worship: Services and Prayers for the Church of England*).

In some circumstances it may be appropriate for the president to say both the opening invitation and these concluding words.

16 **The Peace**
The Peace follows naturally from the Prayers of Intercession and begins the Liturgy of the Sacrament. But this section may be transposed to be the opening greeting or may be used later in the service, as part of either the breaking of bread or the Dismissal. Introductions can be found in the Supplementary Texts and Seasonal Provisions (see pages 290 and 300–329 in *Common Worship: Services and Prayers for the Church of England*).

17 **The Taking**
In Holy Communion the Church, following the example of the Lord, takes, gives thanks, breaks and gives. The bread and wine must be taken into the president's hands and replaced upon the table either after the table has been prepared or during the Eucharistic Prayer.

18 **The Eucharistic Prefaces and Optional Acclamations**
Short Prefaces may be inserted in Eucharistic Prayers A, B and C in Order One. Texts of these are to be found on pages 294 and 300–329 in *Common Worship: Services and Prayers for the Church of England*.

Extended Prefaces may be used with Eucharistic Prayers A, B and E for Order One (pages 294 and 300–329 in *Common Worship: Services and Prayers for the Church of England*). When an extended Preface is used it replaces the entire text between the opening dialogue and the text of the Sanctus. It will be noted that in Prayer E the short text provided on page 30 must be used if no extended Preface is used.

There are optional acclamations suggested for use in Prayers A and F. Those provided for Prayer F echo the style of those in the Liturgy of St Basil and might, especially when sung, be led by a deacon or minister other than the president, then repeated by the whole congregation. Other acclamations may be used.

19 **The Lord's Prayer**
On any occasion when the text of an alternative service authorized under the provisions of Canon B 2 provides for the Lord's Prayer to be said or sung, it may be used in the form included in *The Book of Common Prayer* or in either of the two other forms included in

services in *Common Worship*. The text included in Prayers for Variou Occasions (page 106 in *Common Worship: Services and Prayers for the Church of England*) may be used on suitable occasions.

20   **Breaking of the Bread**
Sufficient bread for the whole congregation to share may be broken by the president, if necessary assisted by other ministers, at this point in the service. The Agnus Dei may accompany this action.

The words provided at the breaking of the bread must be used on Sundays and Principal Holy Days. On other days the bread may be broken in silence or during the Agnus Dei.

21   **Non-communicants**
At the distribution, any of those distributing the sacrament, ordained or lay, may pray for any non-communicants who come forward in these or other suitable words: 'May God be with you' or 'May God bless you'.

22   **Prayers after Communion**
One or two prayers may be used after communion. If two are used, the first is normally a presidential text, the second a congregational text. If only one is used, either a presidential or congregational text is chosen. The presidential text is normally the authorized Post Communion of the day. The congregational text is normally one of those printed in the main text or one of those in the supplementary texts.

23   **A Service without Communion**
When there is no communion, the minister leads the service as far as the Prayers of Intercession or the Peace, and then adds the Lord Prayer, the General Thanksgiving, and/or other prayers, ending with the Grace.

Authorization

The texts contained in this booklet are authorized pursuant to Canon B 2 of the Canons of the Church of England for use until further resolution of the General Synod.

Acknowledgements

The publisher gratefully acknowledges permission to reproduce copyright material in this book. Every effort has been made to trace and contact copyright holders. If there are any inadvertent omissions we apologise to those concerned and undertake to include suitable acknowledgements in all future editions.

Published sources include the following:

The English Language Liturgical Consultation: English translation of Gloria in excelsis, Kyrie eleison, Sursum corda, Sanctus and Benedictus, the Lord's Prayer, the Nicene Creed, the Apostles' Creed and Agnus Dei prepared by the English Language Liturgical Consultation, based on (or excerpted from) *Praying Together* © ELLC 1988.

Thanks are also due to the following for permission to reproduce copyright material:

The Methodist Publishing House: 'We thank you, Lord, that you have fed us…'* (Holy Communion – Supplementary Texts, No. 1, p. 46) from *The Methodist Worship Book* © 1999 Trustees for Methodist Church Purposes. Used by permission of Methodist Publishing House.

The Saint Andrew Press, Edinburgh: for Prayers after Communion no. 3 (p. 46), from *The Book of Common Order*, 1994 © Church of Scotland Panel on Worship.